The Meanest Flower

MIMI KHALVATI was born in Tehran, grew up on the Isle of Wight and trained at Drama Centre London. She founded The Poetry School, where she continues to teach, as well as working as a freelance poetry tutor. She has held a Royal Literary Fund fellowship at City University, London, and a fellowship at the International Writing Program in Iowa. She received a Cholmondeley Award in 2006.

Also by Mimi Khalvati from Carcanet Press

In White Ink
Mirrorwork
Entries on Light
Selected Poems
The Chine

MIMI KHALVATI

The Meanest Flower

CARCANET

First published in Great Britain in 2007 by
Carcanet Press Limited
Alliance House
Cross Street
Manchester M2 7AQ

Cover image: Clump of violets, from an album of flower drawings, with the seal
of Shafi' 'Abbasi, Safavid Iran, Isfahan, dated AH 5 Muharram 1054/14 March
1644. Ink and watercolour on paper. © The Trustees of the British Museum.
Cover design: StephenRaw.com

A CIP catalogue record for this book is available from the British Library
ISBN 978 1 85754 868 6

The publisher acknowledges financial assistance from Arts Council England

Typeset and bound in England by SRP Ltd, Exeter

for Judith and Ruth

Acknowledgements

Acknowledgements are due to the editors of the following publications in which some of these poems or earlier versions have appeared:

Acumen, Agenda, Ashkar Parva, Atlas, Cimarron Review, 100 Poets against the War (Salt 2003), *Images of Women* (Arrowhead Press 2006), *In the Company of Poets* (Hearing Eye 2003), *Foolscap Broadsheets, Launde Bag, Let Me Tell You Where I've Been* (The University of Arkansas Press 2006), *Magma, Modern Poetry in Translation, Morning Star, Nûbihar, PN Review, Poems in the Waiting Room, Poetry Calendar* (Alhambra Publishing 2006 & 2007), *Poetry International* (USA), *Poetry London, poetry p f, Poetry Review, Scintilla, Siècle 21, Staple, The Book of Hopes and Dreams* (bluechrome publishing 2006), *The North, The Other Voices Anthology, The Poet in the Wall* (univers enciclopedic 2007), *The Times, Velocity* (Black Spring Press 2003), *Wasafiri, Women's Work: Modern Women Poets Writing in English* (Seren 2007).

'Come Close' was commissioned by Poetry International, South Bank Centre, and also set to music by Bruce Adolphe in his song cycle *Songs of Life and Love*, premièred in Portland, Oregon; 'Ghazal: The Children' was commissioned by the Barbican Centre and broadcast on Radio 2 *The Word*; 'Ghazal: My Son' was broadcast on BBC World Service 'A Thousand Years of Persian Ghazal'; 'Ghazal' (for Hafez) was included in Oxfam's CD *Life Lines* and a selection of poems is published on CD by the Poetry Archive.

I am grateful to the Royal Literary Fund for a fellowship at City University and to the International Writers Program in Iowa which I attended as a William Quarton fellow in 2006.

Contents

I The Meanest Flower

The Meanest Flower

April opens the year with the first vowel,
opens it this year for my sixtieth.
Truth to tell, I'm ashamed what a child I am,
still so ignorant, so immune to facts.

There's nothing I love more than childhood, childhood
in viyella, scarved in a white babushka,
frowning and impenetrable. Childhood,
swing your little bandy legs, take no notice

of worldliness. Courtiers mass around you –
old women all. This is your fat kingdom. The world
has given you rosebuds, painted on your headboard.

Measure the space between, a finger-span,
an open hand among roses, tip to tip,
a walking hand between them. None is open.

ii

Cup your face as the sepals cup the flower.
Squarely perched, on the last ridge of a ploughed field,
burn your knuckles into your cheeks to leave
two rosy welts, just as your elbows leave

two round red roses on your knees through gingham.
How pale the corn is, how black your eyes, white
the whites of them. This is a gesture of safety,
of happiness. This is a way of sitting

your body will remember: every time
you lean forward into the heart of chatter,
feeling the space behind your back, the furrow

where the cushions are, on your right, your mother,
on your left, your daughter; feeling your fists
push up your cheeks, your thighs, like a man's, wide open.

iii

The nursery chair is pink and yellow, the table
is pink and yellow, the bed, the walls, the curtains.
The fascia, a child's hand-breadth, is guava pink,
glossy and lickable. It forms a band

like the equator round the table. The equator
runs down the chair-arm under your arm, the equator
is also vertical. The yellow's not yellow
but cream, buttery, there's too much of it

for hands as small as yours, arms as short,
to encompass. Let tables not defeat me,
surfaces I can't keep clean, tracts of yellow

that isn't yellow but something in between
mother and me be assimilable.
Colours keep the line to memory open.

iv

Here where they're head-high, as tall as you, will do.
This is the garden in the garden. Here
where they're wild and thin and scraggy but profuse
such as those ones there, these ones here, no one

looking, no one within a mile, you'll find
flowers to pick and to press but before their death
at your hands, such small deaths they make of death
a nonsense and so many who would notice?

with the best ones, flat ones, left till last, take time
to take in the garden, the distance from the paths,
the steps and the terrace crunching underfoot.

Soon you'll hear a whistle. The garden is timeless.
Time is in the refuse, recent, delinquent.
Go as you came, leaving it out in the open.

V

As if they were family, flowers surround you.
As if they were a story-book, they speak.
They speak through eyes and strange configurations
on their faces, markings on petals, whiskers,

mouth-holes and pointed teeth. They are related
to wind. Wind is a kind of godfather, high up
in the branches. They're willing you to listen
to them, not him. Even now you're too old

– though too young in reality for most things –
to understand their language. Once, you could.
You can feel the burn in the back of your mind,

as you hold their gaze, where the meanings are,
too far away to reach. What creature is it
that can stand its ground, keep its mind so open?

vi

There are stars to accompany you by day.
After you've gone to bed, they fall to earth
like dew but, to accommodate that dew,
presumably fall first. You've seen the fluff

from your blanket, a blue cloud in the air;
hooded in your cloak with its scarlet lining,
walking between the pine trees late at night
seen stardust so fine you took it for granted

or took it for vapour, mist, a kind of mistake –
the way a sleeve rubs chalk along the blackboard
and the numbers smudge, x's disappear.

Well then – you've only to turn a midnight sky
upside down to show, when they close above,
the stars below of chickweed, speedwell, open.

vii

The pink primrose flower's an aberration,
a nail discoloured, blood clot on a yolk,
a cuckoo in the nest. How did it get there?
You'd like to pull it out, out from the clump,

beak it like a worm. This time it's an odd one
but sometimes the whole clump goes red as if
some shadow had passed over and instead of
letting it pass, the blooms had taken on

the stain themselves. The yellow ones are true
registers of light and shade but the pink ones,
no matter how bright the sunshine, far away

an overhanging hedge, can never change.
They carry the shade inside them, their veins are blue
and your blood runs cold to see they too can open.

viii

Because you are a child, the earth's dimensions,
of which you know so little, rise to greet you.
Walls, albeit with peepholes into orchards
long abandoned, may be too high to scale

but who would want to scale them when scale itself
and a wall risen up like earth at eye-level
have appointed you like Gulliver to dwarf
the already miniature: ivy-leaved toadflax

mimicking waterfalls, curtaining caves?
The same insect cities you'd see in grass
you now see in stone without bending, stooping,

and your spine is a wall itself. For this,
you are thankful: earth's horizontal shelves
standing, like a glass museum case, open.

ix

These are the things you have made or have yet to make:
six knitted egg-cosies, a sailboat in cross-stitch,
the coronation coach replete with its team
of horses painstakingly cut out and glued,

an apron, a book of miserably pressed flowers,
countless milk-bottle-top pompoms, embroidered
handkerchiefs and one darned for Janet Blue,
all of them neatly and the last passionately.

But materials are intractable
whereas spelling, grammar, punctuation,
bend to the curve of your thought and your thought,

brighter than any needle, magnetised
to their rule, kneels to their rule: a knight errant,
lifting his visor as the Queen's casements open.

x

You're not the centre of the universe
nor do you wish to be. The very thought
fuels your fear of fire, of Joan of Arc
terrifyingly bald, burnt at the stake.

You'd prefer death by invisibility
and diminution, death by camouflage
in florals. You don't think of dying, however,
hovering on the edge of being noticed,

organdie sleeves perked like butterfly wings,
your antennae alert. In later life
you will home in on fields of tiny flowers,

an infant's fading kaftan pinned to the wall,
Annette in an orange shawl, linings, borders,
bindings and trims, each dot, each floweret open.

There was always that familiar ache:
finding your own spot under the trees to read,
the heart always gravitating to love,
still smarting from the last humiliation.

There was coconut ice in pink and white,
between sugar and spice, time to apportion.
You were always fair. When it came to tears,
however, you were mean, a veritable

Scrooge, a Shylock crying out for his jewels
while all the monkeys in the wilderness
scattered and scrambled, gesticulating wildly,

until the savannah, the whole plain, was bare.
What *were* the thoughts that lay too deep for tears?
Oh monkey-child, it's time to lay them open.

xii

I think of Wordsworth's hermit in the woods,
that shrivelling in the heart that leads one deep
into solitude, the longing for it,
as if life were not already too lonely

and a grandchild learning to shred a catkin,
as you once did, no more to be cherished
than her catkin stems. I am entrusted with them:
in one hand, balled, a nest of rusted tails,

in the other, stripped stalks I'll gratefully
chuck from the train. Poetry's on the run.
From exhaustion, the inability

to imagine a larger world and one
too sick to be hurt into words. Be kind,
sweet April, you with your mouth, first vowel, open.

Ghazal: It's Heartache

When you wake to jitters every day, it's heartache.
Ignore it, explore it, either way it's heartache.

Youth's a map you can never refold,
from Yokohama to Hudson Bay, it's heartache.

Follow the piper, lost on the road,
whistle the tune that led him astray: it's heartache.

Stop at the roadside, name each flower,
the loveliness that will always stay: it's heartache.

Why do nightingales sing in the dark?
Ask the *radif*, it will only say 'it's heartache'.

Let *khalvati*, 'a quiet retreat',
close my ghazal and heal as it may its heartache.

Ghazal: Lilies of the Valley

Everywhere we walked we saw lilies of the valley.
Every time we stopped were more lilies of the valley.

Umbrellas passed – fathers, sons,
holding out a hand that bore lilies of the valley.

Every citizen of France
bearing through his own front door lilies of the valley.

But we were out of the know,
though reluctant to ignore lilies of the valley.

Our first May Day in Paris,
knowing nothing of folklore lilies of the valley.

Of Jenny Cook and Chabrol's
buttonhole the night he wore lilies of the valley.

He who sang *Viens poupoule, viens!*
and started the fashion for lilies of the valley.

How fashion then conferred, free
on *les ouvriers* at Dior, lilies of the valley.

Mais nous, sacré bleu, who knew
of charmed *muguets des bois* or lilies of the valley?

And though I wore the perfume
I have always worn before – lilies of the valley

– Diorissimo that is,
no one whispered, 'Meem, *j'adore* lilies of the valley'.

No one made false promises.
And if France did, who blames poor lilies of the valley?

Ghazal: The Candles of the Chestnut Trees

I pictured them in the dark at night –
        the candles of the chestnut trees.
Their name alone made them self-ignite –
        the candles of the chestnut trees.

I pictured them in the pouring rain
as they really are, pink-tinged on white –
        the candles of the chestnut trees.

How many there are and each the same!
same shape and colour, angle, height –
        the candles of the chestnut trees.

Seen from below, most unseen,
they throw no shadow, cast no light –
        the candles of the chestnut trees.

I saw how distance matters more
than nearness, clearness, to see upright
        the candles of the chestnut trees.

Inspired by 'Christ the apple tree',
I looked for a figure to recite
        the candles of the chestnut trees.

Lacking faith, I could do no more
than find a refrain to underwrite
        the candles of the chestnut trees.

As May drew on, the more I saw,
the more they lost that first delight –
        the candles of the chestnut trees.

I've searched for sameness all my life
but Mimi, nothing's the same despite
        the candles of the chestnut trees.

Ghazal

after Hafez

However large earth's garden, mine's enough.
One rose and the shade of a vine's enough.

I don't want more wealth, I don't need more dross.
The grape has its bloom and it shines enough.

Why ask for the moon? The moon's in your cup,
a beggar, a tramp, for whom wine's enough.

Look at the stream as it winds out of sight.
One glance, one glimpse of a chine's enough.

Like the sun in bazaars, streaming in shafts,
any slant on the grand design's enough.

When you're here, my love, what more could I want?
Just mentioning love in a line's enough.

Heaven can wait. To have found, heaven knows,
a bed and a roof so divine's enough.

I've no grounds for complaint. As Hafez says,
isn't a ghazal that he signs enough?

Ghazal: To Hold Me

I want to be held. I want somebody near
                              to hold me
when the axe falls, time is called, strangers appear
                              to hold me.

I want all that has been denied me. And more.
Much more than God in some lonely stratosphere
                              to hold me.

I want hand and eye, sweet roving things, and land
for grazing, praising, and the last pioneer
                              to hold me.

I want my ship to come in, crossing the bar,
before my back's so bowed even children fear
                              to hold me.

I want to die being held, hearing my name
thrown, thrown like a rope from a very old pier
                              to hold me.

I want to catch the last echoes, reel them in
like a curing-song in the creel of my ear
                              to hold me.

I want Rodolfo to sing, flooding the gods,
Ah, Mimi! as if I were her and he, here,
                              to hold me.

Ghazal: Of Ghazals

Ah sweetheart, you have sent me a book of ghazals.
You have sent me a bough and a brook of ghazals.

I have even become tears to live
in your eyes. Let me live in their look of ghazals.

Shahid is dead, great poets dying,
but his swansong is hung on the hook of ghazals.

May the rarest editions of love
bring us both to a shop with a nook of ghazals.

If love's too dear, Mimi, then wander,
penniless, in a long empty souk of ghazals.

II The Mediterranean of the Mind

The Mediterranean of the Mind

i.m. Michael Donaghy

It's not just the heat and sunlight
I love so much in this landscape
as the whiteness of the ground,

glare of limestone, occasional
shells among stone and rubble,
ground feeling lighter than sky

as though heaven were already
here, and real, and detailed.
White dust rims my toenails.

The peaks of the far mountains
are so thick in mist one can't tell
if they are flat-topped or belled.

Villagers, in their mind's eye, supply
the missing crowns, their true shapes,
and cockerels points of the compass.

Everywhere else, death is an end.
Death comes, and they draw the curtains.
Not in Spain. In Spain they open them.

Many Spaniards live indoors until the day
they die and are taken out into the sunlight.
The duende does not come at all

unless he sees that death is possible.
The duende must know beforehand
that he can serenade death's house

and rock those branches we all wear,
branches that do not have,
will never have, any consolation.

★

Playing at house is divine.
What would one do with handfuls
of lavender picked on the hill?

I like the mixture of frugality
and generosity both of the village
and landscape. Lemons have spilled

to circle their trunks and wild
pomegranates silhouette crags.
Small and profuse, white figs,

ripe when they're splitting their skin,
are there for the reaching and
almonds galore that refuse to crack.

Fresh limes too and persimmons,
green on the tree, with the callow bloom
that will still be on them when they're red

and people ill-informed in the ways
of persimmons will eat them,
thinking they're ripe, and pull a face.

They are vessels for jam and properly
eaten only when the vessel's skin
is thin as glass and as clear.

The local delicacy is *turrón*,
'a blending of sugar, almonds,
orange blossom, eggwhite and honey

from bees that have dined solely
on rosemary'. Though how they
police the bees I've no idea.

★

As you'd expect, the morning
was quiet as a church, the doors
and windows shuttered, not a dog barked,

cock crowed, nor did the earth-shaking
tractors (usually one man and his dog
sitting on the hood), trundling

up the Carrer de la Mare del Miracle
under my window, pass. Even
the weather knew it was Sunday,

being chilly and overcast. Then,
as though someone had turned on
a radio at full blast but even more

immediate and loud (I thought
it was upstairs in the little apartment),
a brass band burst into full song.

I rushed to the window in time
to see a small group of followers
vanish round a corner and shortly after

they came again, on the other side,
this time preceded by a band of stout
women in turquoise shirts who handed out

leaflets to the women in doorways,
stopping to chat and laugh. Meanwhile
the musicians stayed tantalisingly out of sight.

Later, I saw a thin girl in red Lycra
with her clarinet and clip-on score
going, I assumed, home for lunch.

★

How joyful the sudden music was.
The whole village sprang to life.
Here, on the quiet mountainside,

I feel like a child, dependent on doors
and windows – or in this case, pines –
for a glimpse of shining brass.

Like flying above a hometown,
knowing your own house is somewhere
down there or passing it by train

behind all the familiar landmarks.
Seaside music without the sea.
Seaside music in a small Catholic

mountain village down in the heart
of the valley and the sound
rising to the very mountaintops.

Earlier in the week, I was listening
to the builders just behind the villa.
For every blow of the hammer,

an echo, more sound than echo
so clear it was, answered back
and where the echo struck

behind the sierra, I imagined
an invisible pueblo growing nail
by nail as the hammer fell

and the echoes nailed them flat.
But the fancy is never as inventive
as reality with its brass bands.

★

Tonight, a gecko is silhouetted
inside the glass of a streetlamp,
every small alternate stepping

magnified as he patrols the pane,
the bulb so fierce and close
it's a wonder he doesn't burn

while outside, circling the lamp,
a bat caught in the light. Today
a *langosta*, camouflaged in greys

on the cane of a lounger, so still
even its antennae were visible,
yet alive. Now crickets are trilling

the seconds, the pulses of night.
Chris talks about Michael
as we sit at the kitchen table.

Michael reciting 'Ode to Melancholy'
and Yeats. Michael and Ruairi
going down to the almond grove,

their voices drifting up from below.
Michael crossing the room, strangely
often, to hug Maddy on the sofa,

how patient he was with Ruairi,
how steeped he was in Lorca.
On the last night, during supper

on the terrace, fetching his flute,
how he played and when everyone
stopped talking, urged them to carry on.

★

Constantly struck by the abundance
of fruit rotten on the branch
or ground: figs trodden underfoot,

kumquats blackened to tar,
whole verges heaped with carob.
The trees themselves sapped of life.

You wouldn't starve here, living
in the wild. But you might die
of thirst, so dry is everything

on the outside but inside, nurturing
juice — thousands of prickly pears
tumbling in swags down hillsides.

You seldom see anyone working
in the fields, save for the little
fearsomely noisy tractors winding

along the terraces. Black lemons,
shrivelled to the size of walnuts,
smell twice as lemony, caramelised.

Occasionally you see a newly planted
rose looking false and out of place
but the fields are covered in a host

of rusted flowerheads and the butterflies
too are rust, orange and brown.
The great burnout happens in June

but in April and May, there's
always the almond blossom
and as early as January, wildflowers.

★

My eyes find it hard to focus —
is it the light? The dramatic rise
and fall of mountains, *barranca*,

the near and far? And my ears
assailed with buzzings and dronings —
even the trees, with barely a breeze,

rattle their pods. I have umpteen
bites. Bites, sunburn, a surface of
innumerable itches and underneath

a sadness for the land and its people,
many of them old and disabled,
leaning on the arms of daughters

who sing as they crawl, arm in arm,
up and down the one street
every day at the same time.

I move quietly through my rooms,
wash fruit and hardly talk
to anyone. *Hola!* I say quickly

to everyone I pass, sometimes
so synchronised with their replies
or mine to their greeting, it sounds like

the same voice, without overlap
or counterpoint, just the one
Hola! between two strangers,

I being usually the younger,
though the children too playing
on doorsteps say hello as I pass.

★

I was mentally tracing the path:
follow the wall – a strange
butter-yellow painted balustrade –

to reach Carrer del Calvari
where the wall gives way to a sudden
very steep flight of steps in sandstone,

on one side planted – and drip-fed
through thin black plastic tubing –
with indigenous and imported shrubs.

The Carrer del Calvari is a white
zig-zag path laid along the cut
of terraces, bordered with pines

and, at intervals, wayside shrines.
Inset, on glazed tiles, the soldiers'
faces often obliterated and gouged,

are the XIV stations of the cross.
My 'study', as I call it, lies beyond
this path in the yard of an abandoned

café under the old Arab fortress
where the children's pool is hidden
by ivy, padlocked, and corrugated iron

makes ticking noises in the heat
like rain; where Spanish fir, Aleppo pines
smell sweet and aromatic, cones

on the topmost branches still fierce
and clinging on, even on those trees
whose spurs are blown away and dead.

★

Everything is quickened by knowing
how short my time is here,
how easily I'll forget it, how

different it will be should I return.
I struggle with the names for things
and even were I to learn them,

whatever the language might be,
they wouldn't evoke – except for me
perhaps – themselves. Today

I have a visitor to my 'study',
an old gentleman in shirtsleeves
who asks how it goes and tells me,

in Valenciano and mime, bunching
his fingers and motioning them
in his mouth, it's time for lunch.

Very Cézanne the whole landscape –
you sense the presence of brushstrokes,
round-headed and flat, almost

the palette knife. But I'd place my words
behind the surface, weaving through nouns,
the undifferentiated but various pines,

into a Mediterranean of the mind
where, like the white *ermita*
culminating in open ground,

some white and holy destination
hoves into view and at the foot of it
one looks, not up, but out.

★

Ermita Sant Albert
is always locked, its tarnished
bell chained and silent.

I look through a small dark pane
like a porthole set in the doors
and cup hands round my eyes

to telescope the dark. A plain,
spartan interior: cloistered arches;
a niche with stucco cherubs, a lace

tablecloth and at Christ's left foot,
a large bunch of dried flowers
jutting out from the shelf; in front,

a table also with a cloth, a picture
and other devotional paraphernalia.
Nothing else. But the big church

in the village square, forever
clanging its bells – heard in London
if you use the public phone –

is fronted by benches and orange trees
where groups of old men sit and,
on market days, middle-aged women.

The padre has been renamed Juan.
He's a refugee from Rwanda
and much loved by everyone.

The side doors are currently a gruesome
shade of brown. It's the undercoat,
we overhear him say at Pepe's.

★

Sitting in the last strip of sun
setting behind the Moorish ruin
I am, having spent all day at the pool,

glad of the breeze and shade.
This is the time I normally leave.
Now, I come to take my leave

of my 'study', the sun, this week
outside my life and the last heat
before the dreaded winter.

Smoke's rising from a bonfire
and through it, the olive terraces
look charred, trunks black and leafless.

The surface I'm beginning to penetrate
seems prickly and sour, despite
a generator's hum, jasmine at the gate,

the old tragic pines with young ones
at their feet, newly planted in rows
with rather unpromising oleanders.

Sounds are isolated in the quiet
much as the trees are in barren soil.
It's not they that grow naturally

out of the soil but the ochre
houses, tile-roofed, earth colour.
I could weep for the flies and the dog

who seems to be barking at his own
bewilderment. But to weep
is to own, is an act of presumption.

★

I do not think any great artist
works in a fever. One returns
from inspiration as from a foreign country.

Every artist climbs each step
in the tower of his perfection
by fighting his duende, not his angel

nor his muse. This distinction
is fundamental. The angel dazzles,
but he flies high over a man's head.

The muse dictates and sometimes
prompts. The muse and angel
come from without; the angel

gives lights, and the muse gives forms.
But one must awaken the duende
in the remotest mansions of the blood.

I'd like to be here in the dark
and look down on the lights of Relleu
rather than up at the floodlit chapel.

Even the stars last night were suspect.
Stars where no stars are, and lightless.
But the moon was bright and legitimate.

I'd like to write with my eyes closed,
blurred as they are with oil.
Behind my lids today at the pool,

I saw the sun as one green light
like a green persimmon. Angel fruit.
A green sun like a green apple.

Almàssera Vella, September 2004

42

The Middle Tone

Seldom do we Andalusians notice the 'middle tone'.
An Andalusian either shouts at the stars or
kisses the red dust of the road. The middle tone
does not exist for him; he sleeps right through it.
                                Federico García Lorca

Just so I spend my life asleep.
Stars, if there are, might shine above
and dust, dust that I've always loved's
now dirt at most I lightly sweep.

But *cantaor*, I too exist.
My middle tone of dung and nectar,
flower and carrion, is a star
that fell, dust I too once kissed.

Al Fresco

Look – there's the thrip on the daisy
too small to see, the spangle galls
on oak, the noonday-fly on walls
basking in my insectary!

And what are these – millipedes? –
strewing the ground like broken springs
while cicadas whistle, crickets sing,
harvester ants sit husking seeds.

Horsefly, housefly, scorpion, bee,
wasps that drowned in the pool but flew,
rosemary flowers I forgot were blue,
I salute you, hesitantly.

Here's ham for you, melon and cheese,
tortillas, tarts, to your heart's content
and for you, mosquito, bent
on blood, gallons to drink as you please.

Summer's on the wing. So, earwig,
locust, beetle and bug, spoil yourselves,
don't stint. Once we've flown you can delve
in dung, in rubble topped with figs.

But when night falls on the floodlit hill,
lacewing, chafer, beware that glass!
Not every window will let you pass.
One light is all it takes to kill.

Scorpion-grass

I travel with groundsel, ragwort, poppy,
seed anywhere and don't look back.
Let any wind sow me, any rough patch be
my home between the cracks.

Forget-me-not call me – if only, if only
memory grew in my tracks.
I blow at a window, away on a balcony,
kick my heels down a cul-de-sac.

The child who stoops to examine me
– my cymes, my sign of the zodiac –
will see, for every star in the galaxy,
there's one in the broken tarmac.

Give me a bombsite, wasteground, masonry,
history I'd otherwise lack.
Shallow my roots but how instinctively
I live without rooting for facts.

Facts are a bind and biography
a woodsman wielding an axe.
Don't give me a plot or a family tree
but a garden swing, a throwback.

I travel with groundsel, ragwort, poppy,
seed anywhere and don't look back.
Let any wind sow me, any rough patch be
my home between the cracks.

Water Blinks

From the height of a child, the shortened height
of a child stooping, massed along wet banks,
opening only when the light grows bright,
all the infinitesimal eyes of blinks
in water seem, not as you might think larger
by proximity, but more like shrinking funnels
a child might feel herself sucked into, emerging
into a fiery wheel of suns until

she knows in a flash how the whole world spins,
stars have their origin in gravity,
just as the budding scientist, impatient
to know how voltage works, becomes – imagines
himself – the transformer and as the current
runs through him, understands electricity.

The Valley

Through a thin spray of flowers from the valley
(and frailer for the shyness you gave them with),
through sprigs of blue, their minute suns, many
and angled to many corners of the earth,
I saw, not the valley or even the hill
that rose in front of me, but half-imagined
plateaux that lay beyond these disused mills:
meadows waist-high, horizons mountain-rimmed.

Wildflowers grow there in abundance, so many
you could reap armfuls of them, cauldrons
of colour stoked with their dyes, cornflowers, teasels
snarling your hair and on your headscarf, apron,
skirt and shawl, the whole sky would spill a pinny
studded with seeds. But thank you, thank you for these.

Overblown Roses

She held one up, twirling it in her hand
as if to show me how the world began
and ended in perfection. I was stunned.
How could she make a rose so woebegone,
couldn't silk stand stiff? And how could a child,
otherwise convinced of her mother's taste,
know what to think? *It's overblown*, she smiled,
I love roses when they're past their best.

'Overblown roses', the words rang in my head,
making sense as I suddenly saw afresh
the rose now, the rose ahead: where a petal
clings to a last breath; where my mother's flesh
and mine, going the same way, may still
be seen as beautiful, if these words are said.

Come Close

'Come close', the flower says and we come close,
close enough to lift, cup and smell the rose,
breathe in a perfume deep enough to find
language for it but, words having grown unkind,

think back instead to a time before we knew
what we know now. When every word was true
and roses smelt divine. What went wrong?
Long before the breath of a cradle song.

Some lives fall, some flower. And some are granted
birthrights – a verandah, a sunken quadrant
of old rose trees, a fountain dry as ground
but still a fountain, in sense if not in sound.

Like a rose she slept in the morning sun.
Each vein a small blue river, each eyelash shone.

Soapstone Creek

The creek sings all night long and all night long
we listen in our sleep, waking from dreams
we recognise as our own undersong
to grief, a gabble of diverted streams

under the paths our lives took, our children's lives
we listened to so avidly but missed
the earliest signs where the ground first gives,
tracks to the water in our own tracks twist,

thinking how blessed we were, wise our choices,
skirting the treacherous silt. Yet all the while
those streams, under the cover of animal voices,
were making a mockery of free will.

Nothing's as constant as the creek. The silence
of the forest depends on it. Our deeds,
misdeeds, omissions too, make no more sense
than rattle-cries, flung where the kingfisher breeds.

Under the alders' canopy that steals
their share of sunlight, understory trees,
spread their leaves as they may, can only feel
sun sideways. And some grow accordingly.

Soapstone Retreat

Late summer sun is falling through the forest.
As if the forest knew it would soon turn yellow,
it shifts a little, stars in the creek below
signalling to the sunlight on its crest.

In the centre it is still. Still late August.
On the periphery, branches, leaves, follow
the scent of autumn. Like a woodfire slow
to get going after the stove's long rest,

the forest stirs with ambivalent longings
for movement, stillness, as if its life were elsewhere
but its heart were here. And as cold nights near,

these last sweet sips at the cusp of the year
hang suspended in the balance as the flask swings,
hummingbird feeds and the sun sinks, stair by stair.

On a Line from Forough Farrokhzad

It had rained that day. It had primed a world
with gold, pure gold, wheatfield, stubble and hill.
It had limned the hills as a painter would,
an amateur painter, but the hills were real.

It had painted a village lemon and straw,
all shadow and angles, cockerel, goats and sheep.
It had scattered their noises, bleats and blahs,
raising a cloud, a white dog chasing a jeep.

It had travelled through amber, ochre, dust
and dust the premise of everything gold,
dust the promise of green. Green there was
but in the face of a sun no leaf could shield.

It had rained that day. It was previous,
previous as wind to seed. O wild seed,
as these words proved. 'The wind will carry us'
— *bad ma ra khahad bord* — and it did.

III   Impending Whiteness

Impending Whiteness

i

It was only in retrospect we knew
it was coming. We weren't thinking in colour,
we were thinking in animal, a new
category of thought and feeling. Dull
as the plates of encyclopedias are,
they were imprinted on our memories.
Comparison was called for and erasure,
and greeting the continents' emissaries:

Bennett's wallaby, Reeves' muntjac, red marmot,
Chinese water deer (solitary things),
mara and peafowl by the dozen roaming
freely through the carparks and cafés, spotted
from the steam train and waved to, then forgotten
underfoot, so fickle are human beings.

ii

It was only in retrospect we knew
how close we were to birth and to the spirit.
Whiteness came as a chick. At first it grew
as a question without our asking it.
Why is it white? we wondered, staring at mud
and the cesspool where the black rhino pissed,
is it male? Does the peacock's tail that floods
more colour than we can bear grow out of this?

We didn't ask, entranced by size and scale
as we were and the picture of a peahen
ushering two plain daughters and the male
heir to her husband's looks into a pen
where the poor rhino, never one to threaten
small children, backed off as they strode in gaily.

iii

It was only in retrospect we knew
how a paintbrush slides from the zebra's flank
down to the shin; how it drops from the blue
to swirl in the depths of a mottled tank
three layers of dapple: cloud, water, seal.
How often have we thought, looking at art,
what is that creature, mythical or real?
Equally, seeing life imitate art,

marvelled at evolution's artifice.
But if the model were extinct, as this
white donkey from north Iran almost is,
we would never have found in Bedfordshire,
from the heart of a Persian miniature,
a half-horse, half-mule, we thought legendary.

iv

It was only in retrospect we knew
white animals, like stones, had laid a trail
behind us: runes from which we might construe
something magical, lodestars that would pale
into nothing. Weather was part of it,
light weakening. And the end of the summer.
And distance, too, that made white tusks hit us
in the eye but the bull elephant dimmer,

a pierced surround for butts of ivory.
The strange became familiar and domestic
cows, ponies, grazing with camels, exotic.
White rhino, no more white than the black are black,
walled a line of oaks and – Rabbit! a cry
shot out while yak announced prehistory.

V

It was only in retrospect we knew,
passing a pygmy goat so white it shone
like a ghost and the silence fell, wind blew
and the trees and grass, with everyone gone,
came into their own, that this place never closed.
We could come in the dark by moonlight, torchlight,
recapture, in the smell of dung that rose
like a flood in the dusk, worlds without sight.

We would be the ones at a disadvantage,
seen but not seeing. We would be as men
and the animals behind bars veiled women,
watching. Matriarchs cornered in a cage,
waiting, waiting for the patriarch's rage.
We would be perpetrators, if and when.

vi

It was only in retrospect we knew
it broke our hearts to hear the howling, see them
moving, an older cub among them, and through
the wire fencing, feel the desire to *be* them,
like them, even the lone wolf wandering,
nose to the ground, in the wood. They seemed at home,
content to congregate on the hill with nothing
to call them further afield, nowhere to roam.

In this country, they died out long ago.
But past the wolf wood, in an open meadow
that took us by surprise as if our worst fears
seen in broad daylight or here, by the glow
of a moon, really were to disappear,
white wolves have lived among us all these years.

vii

It was only in retrospect we knew
it was whiteness everything heads toward.
None of the animals minded us; few
held our gaze but with a tacit accord,
as though we too had a natural place
in the scheme of things, as indeed we had,
allowed us to observe them. But the grace
of lowered necks, lofty horns and ears glad

to obey command words more readily
than children, created an aching barrier,
an invisible veil nothing could tear.
As we headed for the car, solitary
in the carpark, a safari bus roared by
with a bride, waving, throned in the open air ...

Whipsnade Wild Animal Park

Amy's Horse

Amy's horse looked doleful. More pony
than horse, he looked lugubriously
out of his fingerprint eyes at me

from the huge front pane of night.
Outside it was snowing, inside,
orange then green then golden light

flashed through Amy's horse as if
electricity could grant him life.
He had two tails: one short and stiff,

one, superimposed by Amy's friend,
cursive and corrective. Diamonds
glittered in his outline, rainbeads

mapped him like a constellation.
He was a Christmas decoration,
the donkey of our childhoods risen

like a saint on a stained-glass pane.
His eyes were mean and close-set, his mane
a stumpy fringe, his face as lean

as any Christ's but what with the cold,
the crowded bus, the sudden gold
that flooded him, he seemed to hold

not only our eyes but all our anguish,
the terrible burdens of our flesh
and blood, for he had none, no flesh,

no body, nothing but an outline
a finger traced on glass, a sign
for the very naught we can't imagine.

And when Amy's friend erased
what body he had, it recomposed
that naught, ghosting it through the glaze.

The Year of the Dish

It has been the year of the dish.
Like the man who found a button
and had a suit made to match,
for every dish I've been given,

I must re-arrange my kitchen
and, fine as a meridian ring
round a brass celestial globe
as their band shall be, bring

sheikhs to dine on my dishes:
dish with leaves and blossoms,
dish with ewer, grapes,
dish with portrait of Italian,

dish with clouds and lotuses,
dish with ducks, leopards,
dish with fish-scale ground,
dish with two fish, birds

(small birds perched in a grapevine
painted under the glaze),
dish with ship in fritware,
ranged on which my crudités

will hide ship, birds, fish,
leopards, ducks, lotuses
and clouds, portrait of Italian,
grapes, ewer, blossoms

and leaves from their greedy gaze.
It has been, as I said, the year
of the dish. Next year shall be,
I decree, the year of the cafetière.

Motherhood

Suppose I emptied my flat of everything,
everything but my books? The elephants
would have to go. They'd be the first to go
– being the youngest – and the last, the plants
perhaps, relics of early motherhood.
I'd keep the piano, all my files and photos.

I'd keep my grandmother's chest to keep my photos
in, in and not on top of, everything
swept absolutely clear of motherhood.
Nothing shall move: no herd of elephants
proceed down my mantelpiece, spider-plants
produce babies, carpets moths, moths shall go

into the ether where all bad spells go.
I'm sick of the good. Of drooling over photos
that lie, lie, lie, breaking my back over plants
for whom – *Oh! for whom?* Not everything
I thought green greened. Not even elephants
consoled me for the bane of motherhood.

Therefore motherhood must go. Motherhood
must go as quietly as prisoners go
and all her things go with her, elephants
troop behind her, tapestries drown her, photos –
OK photos can stay but everything
dust-collecting goes the way of the plants.

Everything shall live in name only. Plants
now extinct shall be extolled, motherhood
shall be blessed but not mothers, everything
everywhere being their fault though they go
to the dock protesting, producing photos
of happy toddlers, citing elephants,

rashly, as preceptors since elephants,
however vicious they may be to plants
or photographers with blinding flash photos,
are the very model of motherhood.
Such are the myths of nature. They shall go.
There shall be room, time, space, for everything:

room in the wild for elephants and plants,
time to go rummaging a chest for photos,
space for everything cleared of motherhood.

The Robin and the Eggcup

A robin flew into my room today,
into the sun of it, the wood, the plants.

A robin flew into my sleep today,
once for mischief, twice for very good luck.

A robin flew into my soul today,
queried it, rose and flumped against its glass.

So I opened it and the cold came in,
I levered it wide and the bird flew out.

Not for the first time. I let it out too,
my son said, out of the kitchen window.

No! When? Earlier, when you were asleep.
It broke an eggcup. Eggcup! What eggcup?

Not one of those nice blue and white eggcups.
Yes, he said joyfully, I swept it up.

Song for Springfield Park

Because this park is a musical park
and I'm here alone,

because yesterday we found by mistake
any three notes

like all roads led to the very same tune
(Rome in this case

being *All of Me*) and because I said
I like this park,

it's a musical park, I mean the trees
and the curve of the slopes

and you said melodic, I said melodious,
another song

must have stuck in my head. Crookedly, what with
the kids and the crows.

On Lines from Paul Gauguin

How do you see this tree? Is it really green?
Use green then, the most beautiful green on your palette.
And the gold of their bodies God made to be seen?
Make love to that gold and make it a habit.

Use green then, the most beautiful green on your palette
to shadow the world always chained to your feet.
Make love to that gold and make it a habit
to leave love eternally incomplete.

To shadow the world always chained to your feet,
don't be afraid of your most brilliant blues.
To leave love eternally incomplete,
nothing shines more than the love you will lose.

Don't be afraid of your most brilliant blues.
At night phosphorescences bloom like flowers.
Nothing shines more than the love you will lose –
these are lovers' bouquets with miraculous powers.

At night phosphorescences bloom like flowers,
like spirits of the dead in a Maori sky.
These are lovers' bouquets with miraculous powers
where all the colours of the spectrum die.

Like spirits of the dead in a Maori sky
with one eye on lust, one on disease
where all the colours of the spectrum die,
paint, blind Paul, your flowers and trees.

With one eye on lust, one on disease
and the gold of their bodies God made to be seen,
paint, blind Paul, your flowers and trees.
How do you see this tree? Is it really green?

Magpies

I have one tree in my garden
and two magpies in it;
two magpies in a yard
growing greener by the minute.

I have two kids by one father,
three husbands I regret;
the tree that was my grandmother
is dying in my head.

Everywhere is shrinkage
but we've heard it all before;
still trying to count the damage
on old battlegrounds of war.

In black and white, the magpies come,
two heralds in a tree;
in tailcoats and as handsome
as black and white can be.

The first sign of spring is children
yelling in the street;
by *Eid* we will have killed them
before the killing heat.

What season shall we pray for now
when we know what March will bring?
In a mass of green on every bough,
the weapon that is spring.

I have one tree in my garden,
two magpies in it;
two magpies in a yard
growing greener by the minute.

Ghazal: The Servant

Ma'mad, hurry, water the rose.
Blessed is the English one that grows
                    out in the rain.

Water is scarce, blood not so.
Blood is the open drain that flows
                    out in the rain.

Bring in the lamp, the olive's flame.
Pity the crippled flame that blows
                    out in the rain.

Where are the children? What is the time?
Time is the terror curfew throws
                    out in the rain.

Hurry, Ma'mad, home to your child.
Wherever my namesake, Maryam, goes
                    out in the rain.

Ghazal: The Children

The children are not ours
but the child they might have been
   is in their eyes.
The children live in camps
but the freedom they have seen
   is in their eyes.

The children wear boleros,
beads and kaftans, tribal
   paint and feathers,
sandals in the snow and *hejab*
as white as snow whose sheen
   is in their eyes.

The children stand with younger
children on their hips,
   in their arms.
Like animals at grass,
stopping in a day's routine
   is in their eyes.

The children hold belongings –
pens and notebooks, blankets,
   shoes and saucepans;
their fingers tell us stories
and what these stories mean
   is in their eyes.

The children are not ours
but you, Salgado, have brought them
   this close, this far.
I stand within a hand's-breadth
and the world that lies between
   is in their eyes.

Ghazal: My Son

He's wearing a red silk shirt, my son.
He's done me a dreadful hurt, my son.

Now that the devil has shown his face,
he's hiding under my skirt, my son.

A mother is earth, but earth is sick.
A mother's nothing but dirt, my son.

The floor of the gym is strewn with limbs.
Children are lying inert, my son.

I see lights, he says, *hear voices too!*
Obscenities to pervert my son.

Don't look at the lights, the voice is yours.
What can I say to alert my son –

Don't look at the world, a beast that kills,
a savage you can't convert, my son?

What's happened to trust? Don't screen your eyes,
green eyes you always avert, my son.

White roses have buried Beslan's dead.
Mother, don't let me desert my son.

Signal

You'd think that in all this open space,
nothing but fields for miles around
and some cows and trees, you'd get a signal.

Only behind the goosehouse, the roses,
in one of those patches of grass that make
no sense, too small to cross or lie on,

with a sheltering wall at your back, beanrow
on your left, on a triangle of grass
doing nothing and going nowhere,

can you stand and even then, only
with somebody else behind you, wind
blowing their hair and their own mobile

fisted against the rain, with two
or three others besides to bulwark you
– you a child stripping down on a beach,

they a towel or windbreak – do you stand
a hope in heaven or hell of reaching
somebody out there sometime, somewhere.

Sundays

for Tom

i

Together, we have made sour cherry rice,
rolled minced lamb into meatballs and listened
to the radio while eating, him to stall
hallucinations and me to respect his silence,

the time he takes to eat. We've strolled slowly
in the park together, our favourite park,
lapsing into pauses with the falling light –
tennis in the distance – as we slowly climbed

the hill. I've left my shoes at the door, him
reminding me, to scrub off the dogshit later
and now he's at the piano in the nowhere hour
before TV. These are the things that make him

well – company, old and easy, recipes
old but new to him. His playing brings
the night in. Turns the streetlamps on, makes
the kitchen clock tick. Softly a chord falls

and out of the ground grow snowdrops, fat
and waxy, with green hearts stamped upside down
on aprons, poking their heads through railings.
Between his fingers things grow, little demons,

fountains, crocuses. Spring is announced and enters,
one long green glove unfingering the other,
icicles melt and rivers run, bluetits
hop and trill. Everything talks to everything.

How it poured with rain today. My gutter,
blocked and inaccessible to anyone bar
the man with the longest ladder in London,
waterfalled down the window alarmingly.

No, the waterfall is here, under his fingers,
steady wrists, the years of training paying off
in instinctual music; and the fat raindrops, spraying
up like diamanté; and the tailing off

of rain, all the languages of rain, rivers,
gutters, waterfalls, the treble runs
of rain and the bass's percussive beat;
all the liquidity of youth, youth gone

to rack and ruin. How little he ate today
and how much there was to eat – stuffed pepper,
salmon, apple and blackberry tart, coffee.
He can't even swallow his own saliva,

holding it in his mouth minutes at a time,
without hearing them, the voices, seeing
babies streaming towards his mouth, limbs
trigger words command him: that, there, take, eat.

iii

He ate all of it. All of the rice
and all of the *khoreshté bademjan*
– the aubergine dish – I carefully filled
his plate with, not overfilled. He liked it.

He was always sweet about my cooking.
We ate while watching *West Side Story*.
How easy it was to sorrow for Maria
and Tony. Easy to cry and grieve.

Now he's at the piano, today
so tentative but gaining in assurance,
like someone 'learning to live with disability'.
Is he? Or is that someone me?

all of us, all of us who love him.
Joey rings. He's free tomorrow,
Tom's saying – he hasn't decided yet
whether to stay with me a while,

I hope he will. And suddenly
there's sunshine, brightness and a bounce
and his fingers are dancing. Voices
might bedevil him but voices also

save him – Moss's, Joey's, Sara's –
or let him down without meaning to,
without knowing, after they've finished
a call, the music stops again

as suddenly as it started. But now
he's into it – and what's that tune?
coming and going. Tom, what's that tune?
'All the Things You Are' he tells me.

Tintinnabuli

How sad he was, Arvo Pärt,
not to have thanked his teacher
for the parting thought she gave him:

that the biggest mystery in music
is something about – he couldn't
remember her exact words –

something about how to enter
a single sound, just as his janitor,
when asked how should a composer

compose, replied: he has to love
each sound, each sound – so that
every blade of grass would be,

Pärt adds, as important as the flower
(and the bent man on the bent road
picking raspberries, the soprano

holding a green pencil to mark
on her score where to breathe)
and the soul yearn to sing it endlessly.

This one note, or a silent beat, or a moment of silence,
comforts me. I build with primitive materials –
with the triad, with one specific tonality.

The three notes of a triad are like bells
and that is why I call it tintinnabulation.
Tintinnabuli – itself the sound of grass,

blades moving like bells, harebells say,
though there are no flowers but stems alone
and a breath of wind to give the grass direction.

Notes and Dedications

The Meanest Flower

x
Annette in an orange shawl: painting of his niece by Edouard Vuillard.

xi
Shylock: 'Thou torturest me, Tubal. It was my turquoise; I had it of Leah when I was a bachelor; I would not have given it for a wilderness of monkeys.'

xi
'To me the meanest flower that blows can give
Thoughts that do often lie too deep for tears.'
from 'Ode: Intimations of Immortality from Recollections of Early Childhood', William Wordsworth.

Ghazal: It's Heartache

Ghazal: pronunciation of 'ghazal' varies in Arabic, Persian, Urdu, etc. since it is the name of a form and not language-specific. The word is of Arabic origin and means 'talking to women' (women in purdah, with all that that implies). It can also refer to the cry of a wounded gazelle. The ghazal originated in Persia in the tenth century, spinning off from the amatory opening lines of the *qasida*, a pre-Islamic Arabian form of panegyric, to become a love lyric in its own right. Retaining the panegyric's rhetoric of praise, it has continued to flourish since the twelfth century.

Radif: refrain consisting of a word or short phrase which immediately follows the monorhyme (*qafiya*) to close each couplet (although the term 'refrain' can be misleading, implying more weight than the Eastern ghazal would call for). Together, the rhyme and refrain form the binding to unite the otherwise disjunctive closed couplets (usually between five and twelve) which constitute a ghazal. Thematically, these couplets move on a circular plane, from the personal to the political, the meditative to the satiric, rather than in a sequential line of logic, although there are ghazals that observe continuity of thought known as *musalsal*.

Since ghazals are traditionally untitled, the *radif* is often cited for reference.

Ghazal: The Candles of the Chestnut Trees

Christ the apple tree: eighteenth-century American folk hymn.

Ghazal (after Hafez)

Hafez: Khwajeh Shamsu'd-Din (c.1320–1389). In Persia, the secular ghazal reached its apotheosis in the work of Sa'adi, the mystical in Rumi and the two streams culminated in the poetry of Hafez.

The traditional ghazal addresses the unattainable beloved (often in the guise of a young boy or with an ambiguity due to epicene pronouns) and does so from a subservient, submissive position (which obviously poses problems for the contemporary woman poet). This poem attempts an imitation of one of Hafez' most famous ghazals, borrowing his *radif* and staying close to his conceits, but straying from the original metaphors.

The last couplet of a ghazal is known as the 'signature couplet' (*maqta*), in which the poet will claim authorship either by signing his/her name or by using a pseudonym or play on words. If the ghazal represents the world, then the *maqta* is the poet's place in it.

Ghazal: To Hold Me

Rodolfo: Mimi's poet-lover in Giacomo Puccini's *La Bohème*.

Ghazal: Of Ghazals

Quotation taken from Agha Shahid Ali's ghazal 'Of Water' in his last book, *Call Me Ishmael Tonight* (W.W. Norton 2003). Shahid died in 2001 and is much mourned by the many American poets whom he introduced to the canonical ghazal and published in his anthology *Ravishing Disunities: Real Ghazals in English* (Wesleyan University Press 2000). A 'real ghazal' he defined as one that observed the strict requirements of the form. While translating the Urdu ghazals of Faiz, he also asked himself if he 'could make English behave outside its aesthetic habits'. The ghazal in English embodies just such a proposition: but how to use the form without the stratagems of disguise we expect in contemporary formal poetry? Using strict and fully audible rhyme, gratifying the reader's expectation instead of subverting it; employing a syntax that invites the audience to join in the refrain, much like the 'hook' in song lyrics; sustaining a relationship between writer and reader that is an equal one, perhaps sacrificing the reader's pleasure (or irritation) in the writer being always one step ahead – these are some of the challenges.

Dedicated to Archie Markham.

The Mediterranean of the Mind

Michael Donaghy's last professional engagement, and his last reading, took place at Almàssera Vella where Christopher and Marisa North offer poetry courses in Spain. My course started the day that Michael and his family left and, only a week later, we heard of his death. During the days that followed, on a writing retreat, I wrote for him this poem of place, a place so infused with his presence.

Quotations from Federico García Lorca's lecture, *Play and Theory of the Duende*.

The Middle Tone

Epigraph from *Deep Song and Other Prose*, ed. and tr. Christopher Maurer (Marion Boyars 1991).

Scorpion-grass

Forget–me–not: due to its curved stem, also known as scorpion-grass.

Soapstone Retreat

This retreat for women writers in Oregon, founded by Judith Barrington and Ruth Gundle, is where I first conceived this book, dedicated to them with all my thanks.

On a Line from Forough Farrokhzad

Forough Farrokhzad: foremost Iranian woman poet (1935–67). Her poem 'The Wind Will Carry Us' (*bad ma ra khahad bord*) inspired Abbas Kiarostami's film of the same name, which in turn suggested the imagery for this poem.

Dedicated to Aamer Hussein.

Impending Whiteness

Dedicated to the many friends who gave me a calf elephant born at Whipsnade Wild Animal Park for my sixtieth birthday and, in particular, Jacqueline Gabbitas and Martin Parker who took me to see her.

Motherhood

Misquotation refers to Shelley's question, given to Rhoda in Virginia Woolf's *The Waves*: 'I will pick flowers; I will bind flowers in one garland and clasp them and present them – Oh! To whom?'

On Lines from Paul Gauguin

First two lines are quoted in *Gauguin*, Lesley Stevenson (Greenwich Editions 2002). *And the Gold of their Bodies* is the title of Gauguin's 1901 painting of two Polynesian women.

Ghazal: The Children

Salgado: Sebastião Salgado, whose photographs of migrant and refugee children were featured in his exhibition 'Exodus' at the Barbican Centre in London, 2003.

Tintinnabuli

Arvo Pärt: Estonian composer born in 1935, creator of the compositional style known as 'tintinnabuli' (from the Latin for 'bells'). Quotation is from *Arvo Pärt*, Paul Hillier (Oxford University Press 1997). Material is drawn from the documentary film, *Arvo Pärt, 24 Preludes for a Fugue*, directed by Dorian Supin and presented to the International Writers Program by the poet Doris Kareva.

Cover Image

Clump of violets, from an album of flower drawings, with the seal of Safi' 'Abbasi, Safavid Iran, Isfahan, dated AH 5 Muharram 1054/14 March 1644. Ink and watercolour on paper. This delicate drawing of violets may have been inspired by a European herbal, as are many of the images in the same album. The image is reproduced in *Persian Love Poetry*, ed. Vesta Sarkhosh Curtis and Sheila R. Canby (The British Museum Press 2005).